# Reflections on Adoptive Parenting by A Grateful Recovering Know-It-All

# Reflections on Adoptive Parenting by A Grateful Recovering Know-It-All

*Maria Piantanida*

Learning Moments Press
*Pittsburgh, PA*

*Reflections on Adoptive Parenting by A Grateful Recovering Know-It-All*
Published by Learning Moments Press
Pittsburgh, PA 15235
learningmomentspress.com

Copyright © 2017 by Maria Piantanida. All rights reserved.
No part of this book may be reproduced in any form or by any electronic or mechanical means, including information storage and retrieval systems, without permission in writing from the publisher, except by a reviewer, who may quote brief passages in a review.

ISBN-13: 978-0-9976488-6-7

BISAC Subject:
FAM004000 Family & Relationships/Adoption & Fostering
FAM 032000 Family & Relationship/Parenting/Motherhood
FAM028000  Family & Relationships/Learning Disabilities

ONIX Audience:
01 General/Trade

Book Layout:
Mike Murray, pearhouse.com

*Each relationship offers a unique opportunity for greater self-awareness and growth. Seizing the opportunity means letting go of preconceived expectations of what the relationship must be and opening oneself to new possibilities.*

*This book is dedicated to Earl and Rob who have lovingly lived with my ignorance, tolerated my often clumsy learning, forgiven my mistakes, and helped me to grow far beyond what I had ever imagined possible.*

# Contents

| | |
|---|---|
| Preface | 1 |
| The Beginning | 3 |
| Where Do Children Come From? | 5 |
| Family Legacies - Part 1 | 6 |
| What's in a Name | 8 |
| Matches Made in Heaven? | 10 |
| The McDonald's Pumpkin | 13 |
| The Fishing Trip | 15 |
| Magical Moments of Mothering | 18 |
| Invasion of the McDonald's Bowl | 20 |
| Hey Everybody… | 23 |
| Border Skirmishes | 25 |
| The Night Light | 27 |
| What's in a Name - Revisited | 29 |
| What's in a Name - Post Script | 31 |
| Family Legacies - Part 2 | 33 |
| Parental Ambitions | 34 |
| The Return of Big Ears | 37 |
| Sibling Negotiations | 39 |
| Sibling Negotiations - Post Script | 42 |
| Maria's First Law of Parenting | 43 |
| Why Me? | 46 |
| Rob's Kind of School | 49 |

| | |
|---|---:|
| The Experts Versus the Family | 51 |
| The Parable of *The Twisted Tree* | 53 |
| Taking a Chance | 56 |
| Love Is Not Enough | 57 |
| Epilogue | 63 |

# PREFACE

About a year and a half after becoming an adoptive mother, I had an opportunity to co-lead a course for prospective adoptive parents with Christine, the woman who had been the adoption caseworker for my family. As I listened to Christine give information to this group of hopeful, would-be parents, I found myself nodding vigorously, trying to punctuate the truth and importance of her words with my bobbing head. When it was my turn to speak, I would usually end up telling one of my "Robby stories," a little anecdote about Robby and me meant to illustrate the abstract point Christine was making.

On more than one occasion, I would encounter people from the course, months after they had found the child of their dreams. Many of them would comment, "I was thinking about you not long ago. Our child was doing exactly the same thing Robby did. Remembering your stories really helped me keep things in perspective." Encouraged by these comments, I decided to write down my Robby stories.

Over the years, as I shared the compilation of my Robby stories, readers would inevitably make two comments. First, they would say, "There's got to be more to the story." Second, they would ask, "What advice would you give to others who are considering adoption?"

Indeed there is much more to the story. The anecdotes recounted in the following pages occurred from the time my husband and I first began thinking about adoption in 1984 until Robby was in high school in 1990. As I prepare this book for publication, Earl, Rob, and I have been a family for over thirty years and our lives together and apart have continued to evolve. Rob is now in his early 40s and is creating a life that reflects his artistic talents and sensibilities. The experiences that brought him to this stage of life are his, not mine, to tell. Although I have always referred to the anecdotes as my "Robby stories," they are more about me than about him. They offer glimpses into my experience of parenting.

At the heart of so many of the anecdotes is my coming face-to-face with deeply embedded assumptions: assumptions about parenthood; assumptions about myself; assumptions about the way things ought to be; assumptions about the way things are. So deeply were these assumptions buried that I had no idea they existed until some interaction with Robby brought them to the surface. Sometimes the interactions and realizations were funny (or at least amusing). At other times, they were painful. I believe, however, that I am a better person for having unearthed these hidden assumptions and had them tested. I am also convinced that it is only through the mother-child relationship that these powerful lessons could have been learned.

Ironically, I had spent years—first in college and later through reading and personal growth workshops—gaining deeper insights into myself and the world. At the moment I felt I had "put it all together," an 11-year-old boy brought me to the startling and humbling realization that I did not know nearly as much as I thought I did. This brings me to the question of advice.

In short, I have no advice to offer. Advice implies a certainty about what one knows and a presumption that such knowledge is relevant to others. I have no such certainty and try to avoid such presumption. That said, I continue to ponder a number of issues about parenting: choices and consequences, rewards and punishment, family cultures and identity. I offer some brief thoughts about these issues in the Epilogue to my *Reflections on Adoptive Parenting*.

# THE BEGINNING

When I was in the fairly early stages of contemplating parenthood, I talked with a close and trusted friend. After I explained that my husband and I were thinking of adopting a child, she responded, "Maria, you have to understand that becoming a parent is not just a change in your life. It changes your life—COMPLETELY AND FOREVER!" Because I respected my friend's insight into the nature of life, and because her statement held the ring of a fundamental human truth, I nodded knowingly and agreed that it must be so.

In the spring of 1985, my husband and I completed the home study process to prepare ourselves for the adoption of an older child. The eight week course consisted of information about children waiting for placement, introspective exercises on our expectations for adoption, parenting and family, and stories about the adoption experience shared by several adoptive parents. We were very impressed by the thoroughness of the program, conscientiously completed all exercises, and supplemented the formal home study course with extensive reading and informal discussions and interactions with experienced adoptive families. We felt well prepared for our new parental responsibilities and our new family. That fall, my husband and I became the proud parents of a 4'8", 85 pound bouncing "baby" boy.

On November 22 we went to pick up our new son. On November 23 we arrived home. On November 24 our lives turned upside down and inside out. Nothing we had heard, read, thought about or learned had prepared us for the enormous change our lives were undergoing.

I can remember as though it were yesterday, the first day my husband returned to work, and I stayed home alone with our son. About 4:00 in the afternoon, I went to our bedroom, locked the door, threw myself on the bed and sobbed in despair for a good 30 minutes. "What have I done? What have I done to us?" I wailed to the universe.

My despair was not in response to anything my son had done or refused to do. He had been pleasant and cooperative all day. He had entertained himself in front of the television and placed no demands on me, other than a completely reasonable expectation that I would prepare something edible for lunch. No, the despair came from the overwhelming realization that my friend was right. My life had changed—forever. Neither my husband nor I would ever be the same again. For that matter, neither would our son. And none of us had any idea at all of what the future held in store for us as a fragile, newly forming family.

# WHERE DO CHILDREN COME FROM?

No, this isn't a lesson in the basic facts of life. It speaks to the point that in any couple, the idea of adoption will occur first to one partner who will then raise the possibility for consideration. In my case, I was the "dragger," and Earl was the "draggee."

When Earl and I married, we agreed that we did not want to have children. He was already a father of three from his first marriage, and I was a committed career woman with no interest in children. And so it remained for five years, until one beautiful spring day in 1984. I was driving out of the parking garage at the hospital where I worked, when suddenly I started thinking about my father who had died six years earlier. Out of nowhere came the thought, "Who will remember me when I'm gone?" Thus, the seed of parenthood was planted.

# FAMILY LEGACIES - PART 1

Christine, the caseworker who ran our adoption preparation class, admonished all of us eager would-be parents, "Keep in mind that these children will bring different values into your home. These exercise sheets will help you think about what values matter most to you. Think carefully about what you can and cannot live with. Think about whether you can accept and love a child who does not share your values."

My grandparents emigrated from Italy to the United States at a time when Italians experienced considerable social discrimination, a time of ethnic slurs and rampant prejudice. It was a time when immigrants sacrificed everything to give their children a more prosperous future. I never knew my grandparents, but I grew up with their legacy.

From earliest childhood, I learned that education was the most important endeavor one could pursue. Education was the way out of grinding poverty and bitter discrimination. Education was hope; education was the future.

I grew up with stories of my father, dead on his feet, working in the steel mills at night so that he could finish school during the day. Stories of my father sacrificing his dream of becoming a chemist for a practical career as a pharmacist so that he could earn enough money to send his younger sisters to college.

There were stories of my mother's family, too. Her father struggling to get ahead in the old country and having everything confiscated by the newest fascist regime. The family motto, "They (the unnamed forces of evil) can take away everything but what's in here (with a knowing gesture to the head)." I heard stories of my mother and her sisters walking through the bitter cold, riding trains and buses for hours to attend school. It wasn't until years later that I realized how remarkable they had been, four women completing masters degrees long before Gloria Steinem had uttered one word about women's lib.

Education and learning are my family's legacy. It is as automatic and unconscious as breathing; it is as important as life itself!

Being the extremely conscientious people that we are, Earl and I spent hours thinking about and discussing which of our values we wanted our child to accept. We hypothesized at great length about the ways in which our future child's values might differ from ours and whether we could accept those differences. Having analyzed the issue and ourselves to the nth degree, we completed the forms and confidently turned them in to Christine. With a sense of pride and satisfaction, we eagerly anticipated the next step in the process—finding "the right" child for our family.

It would be so good, so rewarding, to pass on my family's legacy; to give a child a chance for an education and for a better life.

# WHAT'S IN A NAME

By the time I married at age 31, I was well past my childhood embarrassment at having a long, unusual and hard-to-pronounce last name. I decided to keep my maiden name.

After some initial discomfort and occasional bouts of irritation when strangers refer to him as Mr. Piantanida, my husband had adjusted fairly well to this non-traditional arrangement. Not until we decided to adopt did our individual names become a source of disagreement. Although we both agreed that hyphenating Piantanida-Novendstern would be cruel and unusual punishment for any child, we vehemently disagreed about which last name our child-to-be should have.

"You," I argued, "already have three children with your name. When we adopt, I want the child to have my name."

"He'll be stigmatized," my husband countered.

"Ridiculous! There are thousands of kids whose mothers have remarried. Lot's of those kids have different names from their fathers." (Including, I might have added, his own children.)

"I don't want him to feel out of place; to have to explain it all the time. He's had enough to deal with."

"Don't be so old fashioned. Kids these days deal with this stuff all the time. It's your issue, not his."

"What's really important to you?" he challenged. "Being a parent or passing on your name?"

I couldn't believe that my normally rational and reasonably

liberated husband had actually turned this into an either/or choice. But I recognized that stubborn set to his face. I'd never won on any issue when that look appeared.

I retreated. "After all," I told myself, "we don't actually have a child yet. Besides, given time, he's sure to see how much this means to me."

Over the next few months, I ping-ponged between two strategies. Operating first on the principle of "if at first you don't succeed," I'd raise the issue. We'd replay the argument and end up back at the artificially created either/or option. At which point, the second operating principle kicked in, discretion is the better part of valor.

As the cycle continued, I came slowly, reluctantly and painfully to the realization that I was seeing a new and deeper part of my husband, a part that surprised and disappointed me. The real choice was not "do I want to be a parent or pass on my name." It was "is this man, this marriage, important enough for me to give up a piece of myself?"

We had known each other for over seven years. It was the first time that we could find no compromise that satisfied both of us. So I stopped raising the issue. I had learned something unsuspected about my husband. I learned something unsuspected about myself. I had learned something about the hidden costs of marriage and parenthood.

# MATCHES MADE IN HEAVEN?

As Earl and I explored the idea of adoption, we met parents who gushed enthusiastically about their "heaven-sent" children. They told of looking through the books that list children waiting for adoption, spotting a picture and just KNOWING in their hearts that this was the child for them. Others spoke glowingly of meeting their child for the first time and instantly feeling an incredibly powerful bond. I heard these testimonials often enough that I began to believe that finding a child to adopt must be one of the truly peak, mystical experiences of life.

Christine, our adoption caseworker, usually had an adoptive parent co-lead the adoption preparation course with her; someone who could "tell it like it really is." One night, Kathy, the adoptive mom co-leading our group, was talking about quirks that adopted children can bring to the family. "My son," she said, "is obsessed with the enormous size of his ears." To hide this mortifying "disfigurement," her son insisted on jamming a ski cap over his ears, and wearing it round the clock. When forced, at times, by unreasonable adults to remove the cap, he resorted to hooded sweat shirts which he always wore "hood up."

During the class break, my husband (affectionately called Dumbo by his childhood peers) commiserated with this mom. The following week, he gave Kathy a snapshot to pass along to her son. (Earl swears this photo was NOT taken to enter him in the Gigantic Ears Contest.) Several weeks later, Kathy was leafing through a listing book and announced, "Hey Earl and Maria, here's the kid for you. Just look at these ears!"

"Ha! Ha!" we responded as we skimmed the accompanying description; then dismissed the young boy as "too troubled." Besides, there had been no cosmic tingles racing up my spine.

Earl and I finished all of the paperwork for our home study at the end of July. As part of the process, we did some "kid shopping"—looking through the listing books and identifying those who looked as though they would fit into our family. We left in early August for a long overdue and well deserved vacation. "Don't expect to hear anything too soon," Christine cautioned. "It can be months before you get a response to any of your inquiries. Try to forget about it and have a good time."

Buried in the stack of mail that greeted us two weeks later was a note from Christine. "Are you interested? Call me when you get back." The note was attached to a sheaf of paper called a psycho-social history. Smiling shyly from the cover sheet was Robby, the little boy with big ears that Kathy had spotted months ago. Call me insensitive, but I still felt no cosmic shivers.

We met Robby with the big ears a month and a half later. A month and a half after that, he came home to live with us.

Occasionally, in the months that followed, I would watch Robby as he sat amidst the clutter in his room, completely absorbed with a comic book or busily transforming one of his toy Gobots. For the life of me, I couldn't imagine him belonging anywhere else. He seemed so at home, so much a part of us. And perhaps, just perhaps, there was an extra electrical charge in the air—a reminder from the patron saint of little boys with big ears that maybe such matches really are made in heaven.

# THE McDONALD'S PUMPKIN

Few social situations are as awkward as meeting one's prospective child for the first time. All of the anxieties of a blind date are intensified. What will we talk about? What will we do? Where will we go? Will we like each other? And worst of all, what happens if we can't stand each other?

In response to these understandable anxieties, a body of practical wisdom for "managing the first visit" is passed from family to family. Take pictures of your home and neighborhood, relatives and significant friends. Try to find out something about the child's interests and take some small gifts or plan an outing to a local attraction. Bring books, games or puzzles that can be used as a shared activity. And of course, plan for a meal at McDonald's, because what red-blooded American child won't be won over by a trip to this favorite watering hole.

We went to McDonald's for lunch. In true McDonald's fashion, the Happy Meal was served in a season-coordinated container, in our case a bright orange, plastic pumpkin. When we returned to Robby's room at the school where he lived, he reverently placed in his newly acquired pumpkin some of his special treasures: Halloween spiders, a rubber snake, stickers of ghosts and goblins, a battered match box car. For the rest of the day, Robby carried the pumpkin everywhere.

As we drove away that evening, I spotted Robby peeking out of a cottage window; perched beside him on the sill was the pumpkin. When we arrived the next morning, there sat Robby on the top step of the cottage entrance, holding the pumpkin. My last view as we left for the airport and home was Robby, standing alone on the porch, waving with one hand, clutching the pumpkin in the other.

The pumpkin traveled with Robby on his first visit to Pittsburgh, and subsequently lived for several years in the rubble of his room. During those rare moments of housekeeping, when under duress Robby would clean his room, the cheerful little pumpkin would inevitably be unearthed from the mounds of books, magazines, clothes, tapes and toys. For a few minutes, at least, Robby would fondly check inside, just to make sure no long-lost treasures were overlooked.

As a result of his cleaning sprees, Robby would finally throw out weeks of accumulated trash. Sometimes he would set aside outgrown toys to be given away. The McDonald's pumpkin was never among the discards. Who knows what insignificant item becomes a talisman of hope, a symbol of promises made, and at long-last, a touchstone of promises kept.

# THE FISHING TRIP

After spending our first day with Robby and finishing our dinner at McDonald's (the second of five McDonald's meals consumed that weekend), we piled into the car, and Earl naively asked, "Well, Robby, is there any place you'd like to go before we take you back to the school?"

"How about, K-Mart," Robby made a tentative cast from the back seat.

In a rare moment of clairvoyance, I saw exactly what was coming and just sat there shaking my head.

"But that's just a store," Earl protested in all innocence.

"Yes," Robby confirmed, testing the waters a bit further.

Earl hesitated, and Robby, sensing the hook was almost in place, said with pride, "It's not far. I can tell you how to get there."

Trapped by the largesse of his initial offer to extend the day's outing, Earl followed Robby's directions, and we arrived at the local K-Mart, where Robby made a beeline for the toy department.

"Oh look, Care Bears!" Robby exclaimed playing out a little line. I surreptitiously checked out the $60 price tags while Robby introduced us to Birthday Bear and Cheer Bear and Grumpy Bear.

"Yes," Earl and I agreed. "Those certainly are cute Care Bears."

Robby sauntered towards the Smurf display. "Look, Papa Smurf," Robby pointed out, gently testing the tension on the hook. "And Jokey Smurf and Handy Smurf." Again, I did a covert price check; we were down to $50.

"Gee, there's a whole family of them," Earl and I said with forced cheerfulness, and Robby with the patience of a born fisherman let the line play out again.

"This is Megatron," Robby instructed us, "leader of the Transformers."

I felt somewhat transformed myself, in an altered state of consciousness, so to speak. With great clarity, I simultaneously noted that we were now in the $40 range, and I suddenly understood why Robby had looked so bewildered, when he had announced with great enthusiasm, "I have a transformer!" and I had responded, "Oh that's nice, do you have a train set, too?" At the same time, I was marveling that the boy, who only a few hours earlier had huddled fearfully in front of us, was now maneuvering with such superb skill and finesse.

"So these are Transformers," Earl and I murmured with feigned interest. Robby moved towards the GI Joes where a large sign proclaimed, "$19.95!"

Until then I had been studiously avoiding eye contact with Earl. Having gotten us into this, he could, I figured, get us out of it.

"These are GI Joes," Robby continued in his tour-guide fashion. "Jimmy at the cottage has one just like this."

"My, what a great action figure," Earl and I exclaimed with false admiration as we turned to each other and simultaneously whispered, "What are we going to do?"

Robby, feeling the hook sink firmly into place, discretely turned his back and played with the GI Joes.

"Christine warned us about trying to buy the child's affection," Earl reminded us with more than a hint of desperation.

"I know. And we already brought him a whole lot of presents," I said out of the depths of my frugality.

"Still, how can we just walk out," Earl said miserably.

Robby played out a little line, easing us in the direction of the Gobot display.

"True." I continued *sotto voce*. "And you did ask if there was any place he'd like to go," I rubbed it in.

"But I meant a park or someplace like that. A store never entered my mind."

With all the smugness that only a self-satisfied wife can muster, I gloated, "I knew we were goners as soon as you opened your mouth."

With the supreme sensitivity of a truly great fisherman, Robby turned and announced, "Look at these Gobots. See how you can change them back and forth."

$10!

"Would you like to get one of those?" we offered.

"Oh, why yes! Thank you." with the most charming smile. "That would be nice." Neatly hooked, deftly played, and expertly landed. All without so much as a single explicitly whined, "Please, buy me something."

Driving back to the school, with Robby happily making Gobot noises in the back seat, I was overwhelmed with admiration. We had come "to check him out." This he knew, because he had been through it before. Yet, he did not play the passive victim. He did some counter-checking of his own. And if we two Yankee strangers proved to be as untrustworthy as all the others, at least he had gotten himself a Gobot for the day's effort. He learned long ago and well, the only one he can truly count on is himself.

# MAGICAL MOMENTS OF MOTHERING

We had learned on our first visit to meet Robby that he gets stomach aches when he's nervous. In fact, when we had first met, he said his stomach was bothering him and he didn't want to go for lunch. Our first clue that the visit might be going alright came when Robby mumbled that maybe he was hungry after all.

Three weeks after our initial meeting, it was Robby's turn to visit us. As I drove to the airport to meet Robby and his social worker, I fondly recalled all the times my mother had met my plane and given me a ride home. "Now it's my turn," I mused.

Bathed in the glow of happy anticipation, I hurried through the crowded corridors and made my way to the airline gate. Having a few minutes to spare, I leaned nonchalantly against a column, smug with the secret knowledge that I was meeting my son!

The arrival of his flight was announced. The gatekeepers opened the door to the jetway. Passengers started to hurry down the ramp. Then he appeared. Tiny, white faced, looking lost. As he hesitantly started forward, I left my post to go and greet him. At that magical moment, my precious little boy doubled over and vomited.

When I tell the story now to prospective adoptive parents who ask about first meetings, I jokingly say, "Well, Robby took one look at me and threw up."

That line always gets a laugh, and maybe over time the sympathetic laughter will ease the nagging tickle of guilt I feel about the split second before I went to Robby's side. The split second of embarrassment when I thought, "Nobody knows I'm his mother. I could just keep going and let the social worker deal with it."

# INVASION OF THE McDONALD'S BOWL

Like other expectant parents, adoptive parents take great pride and joy in preparing a room for their soon-to-arrive child. Clearing out the spare bedroom, painting, choosing furniture—all of these homey, nesting behaviors add to the delicious sense of anticipation. Earl and I were no exceptions.

When we first heard that we had been matched and tentatively approved as parents for Robby, we also learned that the agency responsible for his placement wanted him to move within a month. This meant we had to meet him; he had to visit, and arrangements for the final move had to be set, all of this on top of our work schedules and all in the span of four weeks.

Hectically, but happily, we relocated the den/television room to our unused second floor. Lovingly, we applied fresh coats of paint to Robby's bedroom. Excitedly, we clipped a color picture of the furniture we were thinking of purchasing, sent it to Robby for his approval, and raced out to buy it once we received his "go ahead." With feelings of satisfaction and contentment, we surveyed the results of our efforts. Robby's room was ready for his arrival. We were ready for Robby to enter our family.

We had heard stories of children who come to their adoptive families with little more than the clothes on their back. Therefore, we checked with Robby's caseworker to find out how much stuff he would be bringing with him. It turned out that between Robby's skills as a "fisherman," his well-developed hoarding instincts, and the generosity of his foster family, Robby had a station wagon load of clothes and toys. Upon our arrival home, we carted the bags and boxes into his newly decorated room, and over the next few days, we worked on unpacking and storing things away. "This is great," I mused to myself. "Robby is really here."

My mother, born in the month of September, lived by the Virgo precept, "A place for everything, and everything in its place." I, too, live by that motto. Of course, for me, the right place for everything is in cascading piles heaped on table tops, chairs, bookshelves and the floor. My kitchen is the only place in my universe where truly everything has its place. And, while everything might not be neatly stored in its assigned spot, it could be.

One day, shortly after Robby had moved in, I was in my kitchen fixing dinner. Robby came to me and asked, "Where can I put these?" Looking over, I saw a small, plastic McDonald's cereal bowl and a little McDonald's drinking cup, each cheerfully decorated with Care Bears.

*"What's he bringing those things in here for?"* I thought with a flash of irritation. *"They should be in his room with his stuff."* Then I caught myself. *"Be reasonable,"* I thought. *"Eating utensils do belong in the kitchen."*

Looking at his expectant face, I sighed and said, "Leave them on the counter. I'll figure out some place for them."

Several times over the next few days, I would pick up the bowl and cup and stare resentfully into the cabinet where all the MATCHING dinnerware was neatly arranged: a stack of dinner plates and another of salad plates; bowls in their assigned spot. Glasses as they should be. I would put the McDonald's bowl and cup back on the counter. *"They just don't fit in!"*

One evening my son entered the kitchen and looked at the pathetic little bowl and cup still camping out on the counter top. "Still no place for them?" his forlorn expression seemed to say as he turned and left the room.

My heart turned over. Had I really thought I could confine my son and his belongings to one part of the house, the part where I wanted him to be? Surprisingly, the little bowl looked quite jaunty perched on the top of my plain white cereal bowls. The little cup nestled quite comfortably among the glasses that were, after all, an odd assortment of cups, mugs and tumblers.

At dinner that night, my son happily and proudly took his cup and bowl from the cabinet and used them for the first time since he had brought them out of his bedroom.

# HEY EVERYBODY...

For several years before Robby's arrival, a new Christmas tradition had been emerging. All of my family would gather at my older sister's house in Florida for the holidays. Earl and I would then spend a few days with his mother who lived in a nearby city. As Christmas approached, Earl and I decided to add a few extra days to the trip and go someplace special just with Robby. Feeling that Disney World would be too overwhelming, and wanting to save Busch Gardens for an outing with my younger sister and her husband, we settled on a trip to Cypress Gardens.

At first Robby was somewhat hesitant about this strange place and grumbled as we dragged him onto one of the little boats that glided along the canals weaving through the gardens. Gradually, however, Robby was won over by the intriguing maze of canals and pathways. As he began to relax, he took great delight in dashing ahead, hiding in the bushes and leaping out and growling at us as we strolled by. Caught up in whatever war-game or beast-of-the-jungle fantasies that were filling his head, Robby continued his lurking, creeping and fierce roaring as we left the gardens at the end of the day.

I tried patiently, and then not so patiently, to get him to stop. After all, we were no longer in the relatively secluded glades of the sparsely populated park. Here people could see us.

"Come on, Robby! Walk with Dad and me."

A pounce and a roar.

"Robby, that's enough. We're leaving now."
Robby dropped to the ground, and began creeping around.
"Okay, that's it. We're leaving you."
The stalking menace clutched at my ankles.
Shaking free, I kicked into a high-speed walk and announced to Earl, for Robby's benefit, "I don't know this kid."
At which point, Robby leaped straight into the air, clung to my arm and shouted at the top of his lungs, "Hey everybody, this is my Mom!!!"

Red-faced and mortified, I slunk off to the car wondering what unerring instinct enabled this child to know within four short weeks of living with me that at the core of my being is a painfully shy little girl who equates public attention with profound embarrassment and humiliation.

# BORDER SKIRMISHES

During the home study classes, Earl and I learned that it is very important for parents to set consistent limits for children. Such rules give children a sense of safety and security. The home study process also included many reminders that children will test the limits.

"Okay," I told myself. "First there's a honeymoon phase, when the child is on his best behavior. Then there's the testing phase. And then we settle down and live happily ever after. I can handle that."

To better cope with the testing phase, I began to read books on parenting techniques. "Punishment," I quickly learned is a dirty word. "Natural consequences" is the way to go. Through endearing little case vignettes, the experts showed how arbitrary, authoritarian mandates elicit rebellious behaviors. Reasonable, clearly explained expectations promote cooperation and compliance. If, by some chance, rules were broken, "natural consequences" would help the child see the error of his ways and get back on track.

*"This is great,"* I thought. *"This is the kind of parent I want to be. I can hardly wait to get started."*

When Robby came, we set some basic limits: brush your teeth two times a day, turn off lights and radio at bedtime, get up when the alarm goes off in the morning. Enforcing such simple behaviors became a daily battle, which, in fairly short order, Robby and I had ritualized.

"Robby, did you take your bath?"

"Yes, Mom."

"Here, let me check your hair. It's dry, Rob. Go take your bath."

"Do I have to?"

"Yes!"

"In a little while.

"Now, it's almost time for lights out."

"If you insist,' (punctuated by a disgusted sigh and stomping footsteps).

After one of our battles, I tried to illustrate how much easier life can be when simple rules are followed. I drew a straight line and a circle on a piece of paper. "This," I said pointing to the straight line, "is how some children are raised. It is hard and not much fun always having to walk a straight and narrow path. You are lucky. All you have to do is stay within this circle. See how much freedom you have for running around."

"Yes, Mom," Robby dutifully agreed. Naturally the battles continued. I seethed (quietly and not so quietly) about my ingrate son who, rather than living happily and appreciatively within the circle of acceptable behavior, spent most of his waking hours ramming himself at full speed against the perimeter.

One morning I awoke from an exhausted sleep with the startling revelation that I was expecting rational behavior from a basically non-rational being. His driving force and energy were directed at challenging the limits, no matter how generously I set them. All of my experience, intelligence and education were irrelevant to the primal battle of wills we were waging. The most I could do was nudge him back towards the center of the circle, knowing full well that as soon as I turned around he would be back at the border setting up another skirmish.

It was shortly after that, I suppose, when he asked for the 508th time why he had to brush his teeth before going to bed, that I didn't respond with a lecturette on oral hygiene but actually uttered those dreadful words, "Because I'm your mother, and I said so."

# THE NIGHT LIGHT

I've always admired the television families where troubled youngsters turn to their parents for advice and consolation: Jim and Margaret Anderson offering comforting words on *Father Knows Best*; June and Ward Cleaver charting safe courses through the turmoil of Beaver's adolescence; Mom and Dad Brady skillfully guiding "the Bunch" through the stresses of complicated relationships. These moments of high drama, of intense intimacy, of parental advice wisely given and gratefully accepted were my secret image of parenthood.

After Robby had been living with us for several months, he came to me one night, a disposable, plastic night-light cupped in his hand.

"My night-light's dead," he announced quietly.

"Don't worry," I assured him blithely as I headed from the room to scrounge up another one. "There's one around here somewhere."

I caught a fleeting glimpse of Robby's face and turned back just as he burst into tears. "But it's dead," he cried.

I held him as he sobbed inconsolably. Then, between the sobs came, "Matt and Jenny gave it to me... I had it at their house. . They gave it to me before I left."

The sobs turned into a keening wail. "And now it's dead."

Matt and Jenny, the foster parents who had given him refuge when protective services had taken him from his birth family. Matt and Jenny who had given him love and more stability than he had ever known in his eleven years. Matt and Jenny who had said goodbye and sent him to a strange new family in a faraway state with a protective totem—a disposal, plastic night light. Now it was all dead.

As the sobs subsided, I said, "Robby, do you remember that watch box you got from Dad a few weeks ago?"

A forlorn nod.

"Why don't you find it and put the night light in there? It will have a special resting place, and you can keep it for as long as you want."

He wiped his eyes, began rummaging through the clutter in his room and, after several minutes, unearthed the velvet-covered box. Reverently, he placed the night light in the box and gently shut the lid. He slept with the watch box that night and several nights thereafter.

Periodically, Robby comes across the watch box. "What's this?" his expression seems to say as he snaps it open. As the contents are revealed, the look of expectancy fades and his face becomes pensive. For several minutes, he gazes quietly at the totem from his past, then tenderly closes the box and places it carefully in a desk drawer.

Watching this scene, I remember how close I had come to missing the signal. There had been no television family scenario. No tentative knock on the door. No clearly articulated, "Mom, I have a problem. Can we talk?" No insightful questioning and skillful guidance. I have yet to experience any scenario that remotely matches my secret, TV-inspired fantasy of parenthood. But I count that instant, when a fleeting impression pulled me back from the brink of practicality, as one of my finest moments of parenting.

# WHAT'S IN A NAME – REVISITED

During our adoption preparation classes, my husband and I had learned that older children often have very mixed feelings about changing their name. On one hand, it is part of their identity. Giving up their name may represent giving up some part of self or may feel like a betrayal of their birth family. (Tell me about it!) On the other hand, taking the adoptive family's name can strengthen the sense of bonding and belonging for children who have floated through a system calling no place home and no one family.

Earl and I were determined to be sensitive to this issue. So after Rob arrived, we found ourselves once more dealing with the issue of names. I still couldn't entirely let go of the hope that Earl would come to his senses and let Rob take my last name. So we recycled our standing argument a few more times with no change in the bottom line.

"Okay!" I finally suggested. "How about this? We let him keep his birth name."

My husband blanched.

"No, seriously." I said with perverse glee. "It's fair. Think about the reactions we'll get when we introduce ourselves."

"That's exactly what I'm thinking about," Earl said, standing firmly on the unshakable ground of "what's best for Robby."

As the time drew closer for us to file the papers to make the adoption legal, we did try to sound Robby out about keeping or changing his name. Each time, he responded with vague disinterest, until the week before we were scheduled to appear in court. Then he hinted obliquely that maybe he didn't want to give up his name. When we tried to discuss his feelings directly, he backtracked toward studied indifference. There was no time left to "work it through" as the psychologists and social workers would say.

A week later, our son sat dwarfed in the witness box of an immense courtroom. The judge studied the adoption petition for a few moments, then peered over the massive mahogany bench and asked Robby, "What's your name going to be?"

"Robert A\_\_\_\_ M_____ Piantanida Novendstern," he replied clearly and proudly.

"I'm glad you said it and not me," the judge chuckled. Rob chuckled, too. So did Earl. So did I.

# WHAT'S IN A NAME – POST SCRIPT

Several months after we had legally finalized the adoption, I was relaxing on the couch reading a trashy novel. Rob came into the room, sank down to the floor by my side and announced, "Mom, remember when you and Dad asked me about what name I wanted. Well, I've been thinking about that a lot, and I've made a decision."

*"Here it is,"* I thought to myself. *"The moment of identity crisis. The moment they'd warned us about"* I took a deep breath, put down my book and said in the most neutral voice I could muster, "Yes, what have you decided?"

"I want it to be Davey Jones," he pronounced solemnly.

"Davey Jones!"

Suddenly, images from the past several weeks flashed through my mind: the obsessive need to be home for his FAVORITE television show, the Cockney accent my son had been mimicking, the haunting melody from the family room, "Hey, hey, we're the Monkees."

"Sorry, son. The paperwork's filed."

"But, Mom!!!"

"Forget it. If you want to shell out the money for a lawyer and a court hearing when you're 18, be my guest. Until then, you're stuck with the name you've got."

Shoulders slumping with disappointment, he dragged himself to his feet and sulked out of the room.

So much for sensitivity. So much for empathy. So much for identity crisis.

Over the next few years, as one FAVORITE television show replaced another, Rob periodically declared, "I don't care what you say. When I'm 18, I'm changing my name!"

"To what, son?"

"Scotty!" (complete with Scottish burr during the *Star Trek* phase).

"Rob Raintree!" (with a western twang during the *Young Riders* phase).

Well, maybe the experts are right about the importance of names to older adopted children. After all, hero worship is an experimental search for identity.

# FAMILY LEGACIES - PART 2

John Dewey, one of the most influential philosopher/educators in the United States, wrote a book, *Experience and Education,* in which he makes a distinction between educative and mis-educative experiences. According to Dewey, experiences are educative when they set the conditions for further growth and development; in essence, they foster the individual's desire to go on learning. Mis-educative experiences undermine the desire for learning and shut down the overall growth process.

When Robby first came to live with us and we would take him on outings, he would get what I called his "haunted look." He would turn ghostly pale and appear to see nothing, hear nothing and care about nothing except returning home and collapsing in front of the television. There he would remain for hours, curled in his bean bag chair, absorbed in cartoon shows and superhero movies.

Over time, the haunted took disappeared, but even now Robby never truly looks forward to new experiences. He sees the world as dangerous and threatening; he "knows" that new people, places and activities will cause him some unnamed, but expectable misery.

Robby, like me, carries a legacy about learning from his birth family. His legacy was shaped by the mis-educative experiences of his early years. Experience is painful; learning is irrelevant; escape through fantasy is, literally, as important as life itself.

# PARENTAL AMBITIONS

The experts explain that children who have been removed from their birth families and bumped through several foster homes before adoption, frequently experience developmental delays. Translated into simple English, this means they act younger than their age. In one sense, this is positive. Once these children feel safe in their adoptive family, they often regress in an unconscious effort to reclaim their right to basic care and nurturing, a right from which they had been cheated. In a less positive sense, developmental delays are indicative of deprivations that are so great they may never be overcome.

During the optimistic days of the home study classes, when Earl and I were busily writing out our reasons for wanting to adopt an older child, I naively believed that one of our satisfactions as parents would be helping a child overcome his developmental delays. With all the resources we were willing and able to provide, our child would be able to "catch up" and reach his full potential.

One cold February evening, my husband and I attended a dinner with a group of my husband's colleagues and their wives. I was seated next to a lovely, bright, articulate woman who is obviously a very caring mother. Most of the conversation focused on her children. The oldest was attending a prestigious engineering school, was carrying a heavy load of credits and had a cooperative work-study position in a large, well-regarded company. As a student, he was making $2,000/month. This proud mother talked with enthusiasm about her son's excitement, accomplishments, and his plans to complete his bachelor's degree and get a well-paid entry level engineering job upon graduation. Her middle son was finishing his last year in high school. He had reluctantly agreed to go to college, but knows he will return to their community and go into the landscaping business. And oh yes, he plays hockey on the Amateur Team of a major hockey franchise, last year ranked in the top ten players in the league, and even though he's basically a home-body, he had traveled extensively last season to play in hockey games. Her daughter, a 13-year-old who I knew from an earlier meeting is absolutely gorgeous, was passionately into horses. Since the previous spring she had owned her own thoroughbred and was already well into jumping him in indoor arenas. She was learning cross-country jumping, and had taken first place the first time she showed the horse.

At some point, about an hour and a half into the dinner, this proud mother asked me, "You have one son, don't you? How old is he, about 14?

When I confirmed this, she asked, "Well, then he must be into sports. What does he like to play?"

"Actually," I replied, "he hates any kind of organized team sports. He's really into fantasy. He also likes to draw, and is talking about being a cartoonist when he grows up."

My dinner companion then launched into a description of the Discovery Program available in her children's school district. They offer a cartooning class, computer lessons, sewing, art, in short, a whole array of leisure learning classes that would delight any wholesome, high achieving, upwardly mobile adolescent. Her daughter, of course, had already completed robot building, sewing, and was now into tie-dying.

As this woman talked, all I could think of was my son, dressed in a flowing cape he had purchased at Halloween, leaping down stairs, bounding over furniture and proudly declaring, "Guess who I am."

"Superboy," I respond dutifully.

"That's right," he smiles as he pretends to tear off his "Clark Kent" clothes and fly off to battle Lex Luther.

I guess that's what the experts mean by developmental delays.

# THE RETURN OF BIG EARS

T he experts in adoption like to talk about claiming behaviors, things that adults and kids say and do to create the parent-child relationship, which, in a birth family, is taken for granted.

One night as Rob was getting ready for bed, he turned to me and announced, "I hate my ears! They're big, and they stick out too far."

"No they aren't. They're cute." I said in my most reassuring voice.

Unswayed, Rob insisted, "They are, too. And I hate them."

"Well," I conceded, "maybe they were a little big for the size of your head when you were younger. But your head's grown. They look fine now."

"I hate them!" cried Robby bursting into tears.

Even when Robby first came to live with us, he did not cry easily or often. But a few times, like the evening of the dead night-light, and now, he cried with the high pitched wail of an abandoned infant. None of my efforts to comfort him penetrated his primal desperation. After a long, long time, the wails trailed off to sobs, and sniffling, he moaned, "Why can't they be like yours?" Sitting up, he said, "See, see how yours lie flat against your head. I wish I was born to you so I could have ears like that."

A claiming behavior! As clear and classic an example as any expert ever gave in any textbook. Unfortunately, the experts never said whether it would help my son or hurt him, if I admitted that it was his big ears that had brought him to the family he was in the throes of claiming.

# SIBLING NEGOTIATIONS

Rob had several birth siblings, and all but one brother had been adopted. Not long after Rob came home, we visited Jordan and took him out for lunch. As we sat in (where else) McDonald's, Jordan dismantled and consumed his quarter-pounder layer by layer. As he popped a pickle into his mouth, he looked up at us with the most incredible brown eyes and asked, "Why don't ya'll adopt me, too?"

My heart broke. How do you explain to two young boys that social workers felt they both had a better chance of healing and growing in separate families?

So for several years we were haunted by periodic requests. "Adopt my brother."

"Rob, you know we can't do that."

"Well, then adopt me a different brother."

"No. That's not something we're willing to do."

Finally, after Jordan was adopted into his own family, he and his adoptive mom came for a visit.

The weekend went pretty well, although Rob's activities and freedom were curtailed to match his younger brother's need for stricter limits and greater supervision.

At the end of the visit, as we drove away from the airport parking lot, Rob announced from the back seat, "Mom, Dad! Remember when I wanted you to adopt me a younger brother?"

"Yes," we said in unison.

"Well forget it! I like being an only child just fine!"
Round #1 to the parents!

※

I was sitting in my office one afternoon, absorbed in my work, when the phone rang.

"Mom! Mom! You'll never guess what!"

"So tell me, Rob, what is it?" I asked, amazed by the excitement bubbling through Rob's usual reserve.

"It's the best news ever. You know the house down the street from us?"

"Which one?"

"The lady there has two cats, and she said I could have both of them!"

With a sinking feeling I said, "You're forgetting, Rob. I'm afraid of cats."

"But they're free. She said I can have them for nothing."

Never had I heard so much enthusiasm in his voice. It killed me to say, "Rob, listen. I'm afraid of cats. Remember."

"Oh…" the enthusiasm died away to desolation.

"I'm sorry, honey. But I just can't live with a cat. Why does this lady want to give them away anyway?"

"She says they're mean."

Round # 2. Technical advantage to Mom. Psychological advantage to Rob.

※

Inevitably, several months later, Rob piped up, "What about a dog?"

"Yes, what about a dog?"

"Why can't I have a dog? You're not afraid of them?"

"True. But I'm not an animal person. I don't like animals. I especially don't like animals in the house. Forget it!"

"But why not? You have Dad. Dad has you. Who do I have?"

"You have the two of us."

"It's not the same. I want someone special of my very own," Rob persisted.

I brilliantly countered his every argument. I pointed out the disadvantages, the hard work, the responsibility, the loss of freedom. I was clever. I was witty. I was adamant. Yet I knew in my heart, the battle was over. Rob had won this round the day he had called about the cats...the day his voice had finally been filled with the unbridled excitement I had longed for him to experience...the day it had been me, not some awful birth parents, who had dashed his hopes.

I held out for a few more months while Rob and I parried back and forth on the details of a "contract." A friend of mine who was involved in an animal rescue group called Adopt-A-Pet, became our caseworker. "The group," she explained, "needs foster homes where stray animals can be kept until a permanent home is found."

"Alright," Earl and I conceded. "We'll give you a chance to prove you can take care of a pet."

"No problem," Rob responded.

"That means everything. Feeding—"

"Sure, sure," Rob said.

"Walking."

"Right. Right."

"Taking her out to—"

"Mom, I know. I know. It's not a problem. Trust me."

"Right, son."

One day, we went "just to see" a couple of dogs who needed foster homes. "Remember," we cautioned Rob, "we're not going to pick a dog. We're just gathering information."

The next day Sparky came home to live with us.

# SIBLING NEGOTIATIONS – POST SCRIPT

One day shortly after Sparky joined the family, I came home from a long, hard day of meetings. There was Sparky, dancing and panting with joy at the mere sight of me. She hopped and yelped until I opened the baby gate that restricted her to the sun-room during the family's absences. Bounding in excitement, she couldn't wait to reach me, leap up and give me a welcoming hug. "What," her bright eyes seemed to say, "can I do to please you? Just tell me, and I'll do it!"

Suddenly it hit me.

"You know the difference between adopting a dog and adopting a boy?" I asked Earl as he came through the door later that day.

"No, what?" he sighed.

"The dog is grateful!"

# MARIA'S FIRST LAW OF PARENTING

When we first read Robby's psycho-social history, we were impressed by the comment, "Robby is a bright young man who has the potential for going on to college. We hope to find a family who can help Robby pursue his education." Was this the kid for me, or what!

Unfortunately, Robby had missed a lot of school during his early years and his unsettled life had made it difficult for him to concentrate on learning. Robby's social worker recommended that we enroll him in a special education school for a year or two. It was her hope, and ours, that the supportive and protective environment of a special education school would help Robby to make up for all the years of sporadic schooling. He would be socialized into the world of school and develop "school appropriate" behaviors like listening to teachers, taking notes, completing assignments, studying for tests. Each time we had a parent-teacher conference, however, I lost a little more hope and faith that these changes were taking place.

After two years, Earl and I began pushing to have Rob mainstreamed—i.e., integrated into regular classes. After much persistence, we finally got the school to agree to a split schedule. Rob would spend his mornings at the special education school and his afternoons at the regular junior high school. Delighted, Earl and

I breathed a sigh of relief and waited for Robby to "take hold" at the regular high school.

"Well, Rob, how did school go today?" we asked with hearty enthusiasm.

"Ok."

"Did you meet any kids?"

"A few."

"How was lunch in the cafeteria?"

"My bus got there late. I ate lunch in the counselor's office."

"How were your classes? Do you have any homework?"

"Not really. I'm going to watch some TV now."

Not a glowing report, but Rob needs time to warm up to new situations. "Don't push too hard, we reminded ourselves."

But as the days grew into weeks, our desperation mounted. He never brought home any assignments, or books for that matter. When we tried to institute a homework checking procedure, he constantly had excuses. His books were at one school, his notes at the other. Mrs. H. said he had to do homework; Mr. L said he didn't. With each excuse, my impatience grew. "For heaven's sake," I fumed. "All he has to do is put the damn stuff in his back pack and carry it with him."

"Calm down," Earl urged. "He's still getting adjusted."

"Adjusted to what?" I ground out between clenched teeth. "It's not like we ask him to do that much. Just go to school and manage his school work. What's the big deal?"

Weeks grew into the first grading period, and Rob's report card came home with Ds and Fs. "Look, just look at that," I virtually exploded with righteous indignation. "I just knew he's been goofing off. I can't stand this…"

My tirade continued for days, fueled by the tangible evidence of Rob's "blowing off school." It took Earl, our family therapist, Rob's teachers and counselors to finally bring my rantings and ravings to an end. "You have to have reasonable expectations," they reminded me in tones of calm rationality that grated on my raw nerves.

"Look," I stated in a tightly controlled voice, "what's so unreasonable about this. He gets up in the morning. He makes sure his books and lunch are in his back pack. He gets on the bus, spends the morning at one school. Gets on a second bus and goes to the Junior High. Puts his books, assignments, notebooks, and pencils in his back pack at the end of the day and comes home. What's so hard about that? What's so unreasonable?"

While Rob was attempting his transition at school, I, too, was making a transition. I had quit my full-time job in one university department and taken a part-time position in another so that I could pursue my dream of becoming a consultant. However, I had agreed to finish up some loose ends at my former job until they could hire a replacement. So I spent my mornings in one office and my afternoons in an office across campus. As was the style, I wore Reeboks and sweat socks for my daily commute, changing into presentable high heels when I arrived at my office.

I formulated Maria's First Law of Parenting the day I had to apologize repeatedly to business associates, "Please, excuse my tennis shoes. Right now I'm going back and forth between two offices. I got confused and forgot my real shoes at home."

Maria's First Law of Parenting: "The more vehemently you chastise your child for some perceived failing, the greater humiliation you will suffer upon making exactly the same mistake!"

Shortly thereafter, we ended the mainstreaming experiment and let Rob return full-time to the special education school. The final touch of cosmic justice arrived after the school-year ended when we met a teacher from our local school system. "The junior high was a mess last year," he explained. "It was the first year of their reorganization and nobody knew what was going on. Teachers couldn't get books and supplies; the kids hardly knew each other; the principal barely knew any of the staff." Into this chaos we had sent our son who hates change even under the most pleasant of circumstances. I felt about two inches tall.

# WHY ME?

Individuals who have suffered traumatic childhoods must come to terms with the pain of their past. Experts in adoption suggest that uprooted children never completely resolve the incomprehensible twists of fate and circumstance that caused them to lose their birth families. The term, "reconciliation" has been suggested as a more appropriate term to describe the often life-long process of reworking and accepting the loss. In the case of children who have been abused and neglected, they must also reconcile the lost innocence of youth. Rob, to put it mildly, had a lot of early experiences to reconcile. On the advice of his caseworker, we entered into family counseling almost from the week that Rob came to live with us.

Most of the time, Rob steadfastly maintained the position that his past life was behind him, and he didn't need to dwell on it. To all appearances, he used his therapy sessions to play with GI Joes, transformers and other fantasy figures the therapist kept on hand as therapeutic tools. He disparaged the group counseling sessions at school as a "stupid waste of time," and occupied himself with the more meaningful pursuits of watching television and acting out fantasy games with his friends in the neighborhood.

One Sunday when Rob had been with us for about three years, we were driving home from church.

"Well, church school wasn't as boring as usual," Rob offered from the back seat.

"Oh," Earl and I responded in unison, "what happened?"

"We were talking about abortion and adoption, and I told them if they wanted to know about adoption they could just ask me!"

"What did you tell them," we asked, holding our breath.

"I told them that my mom knows a lot about adoption and has studied a lot, but that I, no offense, Mom, am the real expert."

Rob proceeded to recap for us what may have been a 45 minute monologue on the subject of adoption. I was astonished by his insight; not only into the adoptee's experience, but also the adoptive parents' and even the birth family's perspectives. When Rob finally finished his back seat recitation, I asked, "What did the other kids think about all this?"

"They wanted to know why kids get taken away from their families."

"What did you tell them?"

"In my family, it was like riding a Port Authority bus. You know how every time the bus stops, more people crowd on?"

"Yes."

"Well, that's what my birth family was like. The babies just kept coming and coming until my family couldn't take care of us anymore."

I was speechless.

"They also asked what it was like meeting people who might adopt you."

"Wow, how did you answer that one?"

"I told them it's like being in the vegetable section of the supermarket. You know how people go to the vegetable section, and they'll pick up a cabbage and inspect it." In the rear view mirror I could see Rob carrying out the gesture, turning the imaginary cabbage this way and that, looking for the flaws.

"Some people decide they don't want that head of cabbage and put it back on the stand," he continued, relishing the nuances of his metaphor. "Finally some people come along, pick it up and decide the cabbage is good enough. They take it home with them." He ended with a hint of amused irony in his voice that seemed to imply, "So much for the idiots who didn't recognize a good thing when they saw it."

For all those years I thought he had been in denial, resisting therapy, and hiding out in his fantasy world. Somewhere, somehow he had been reconciling the fragments of his life. What could we say. Truly, Rob was the expert.

About a year after the Sunday school episode, Rob must have been working through another cycle of reconciliation. This time he raised the other side of the "why me" question. Not "Why did this have to happen to me?" But "Why did you choose me? Why of all the children out there, did you pick me?"

This time, I told Rob the story of "big ears." And if he was as mystified as I am that such momentous life events can turn upon such seemingly insignificant circumstances, he gave no indication of it. Not long after that, however, he did mention a theory of his, one that he had expounded to friends in his science class. "The reason I can hear so much better than a lot of other people," he told them, "is that my ears stick out further, and so they catch more of the sound waves."

# ROB'S KIND OF SCHOOL

As time went on, Earl and I became more and more convinced that Robby's special education school treated him like an academic throw away, never really expecting him to learn, to develop study skills, or to continue his education beyond high school. They focused almost exclusively on controlling inappropriate social behaviors, and seem to believe a token high school diploma would be good enough.

After the disastrous results of our previous mainstreaming effort, Earl and I began to explore alternatives to our school system's senior high. In time, we found a small, academically-oriented, alternative high school with a tremendous track record in working with underachieving students. We were impressed with its emphasis on learning rather than schooling (a seldom appreciated but extremely important distinction) as well as its philosophy of customizing the educational program to the needs of the student.

Fearfully, Rob agreed to visit. By the end of two hours his anxiety had evaporated. "This is my school," he declared as we got into the car. "This is where I want to go next September."

"So you liked it," I said, carefully masking any signs of triumph.

"Yes! I can't believe it. Students get to go out to Squirrel Hill for lunch. They call teachers by their first names. One kid even swore in class and nobody yelled at him. This is where I want to go."

"Well you know," I cautioned, "you have to take studying seriously here and prove that you can be responsible."

"Oh sure, sure," he said. "Did you see, they had vending machines where the kids can get snacks between classes!"

"Patience," I tell myself. "Just let him get here first. He'll find out about the work and the expectations that go along with the freedom and privileges once he gets here."

But despair and desperation welled up inside of me. Won't he ever realize how important an education is? He has so much catching up to do. There is so little time. He's so bright. It's such a waste.

# THE EXPERTS VERSUS THE FAMILY

Having gotten Robby's tentative agreement that he might actually be willing to attend this new school, Earl and I dutifully went off to meet with the special education experts. We described the school to them and explained our plans to enroll Robby for the next school year. "But Robby isn't ready!" they objected. "He needs another year here so we can prepare him."

"Was this another one of my unrealistic and unreasonable expectations?" I thought to myself. "Am I trying to push too hard? Am I setting him up for failure?"

Earl and I decided a second opinion was called for; a second opinion from someone who didn't know Robby, but who could look at his history and see how far he'd come. Someone who could administer all the right tests and "objectively prove" that Robby was more capable than the school personnel wanted to believe. Robby met with a psychologist who specialized in evaluating children's IQ, thinking capabilities, and personality. He spent several hours completing a battery of educational and psychological tests. Several weeks later, filled with hope, Earl and I went to learn the results of the evaluation.

As the psychologist explained the test scores to us, I became more and more upset. It seemed to me she was stripping away my son's strengths, his capabilities and his humanity. The image of a stunted, barren tree came to me, and once I saw this internal vision, I could barely maintain my composure until I could escape from the psychologist's office.

I cried almost constantly for the next three days. Were my son's sense of humor, his brightness, his affection an illusion? Was I deluding myself about his abilities? Were my expectations and hopes for him too high, too unfair? Did the tests reveal the TRUTH about my son, a truth I wanted to deny at his expense? Or, did the tests dissect him into such tiny pieces that his strengths oozed away in the process?

As I agonized with self-doubts and with concern for my son's welfare and future, a second image emerged. I thought of the lone cypress tree that grows on a sheer cliff on the California coast.

# THE PARABLE OF
# *THE TWISTED TREE*

Once there was a very small tree. By some strange chance, it had sprouted in rocky soil on a cliff high above the ocean. Day and night, the strong sea wind blew against the little tree, making it very hard for the tree to grow. Sometimes seagulls would sail by and come to a gliding rest on the sandy patch of ground right next to the tree. On those occasions, the little tree would beg in a very pitiful voice, "Please, seagulls, help me escape from this windy, rocky place. Growing here is such hard work, and I get very tired."

But the seagulls just screeched and laughed and flew away, leaving the little tree alone. It was hard to tell whether the salty brine glistening on the tree's bark came from the ocean spray below; but of course it must, because we all know that trees can't cry.

As the years passed, other birds would come and perch on the tree. They sang songs of faraway forests where giant trees grow hundreds of feet right up towards the sun. "You should be more like your cousin trees," the birds would scold. "Their trunks are straight, and they stand very tall, like proud soldiers."

"I can't!" cried the little tree, and the birds would shake their heads and chirp with regret.

Still more years passed, and even though he thought at times it would be easy to give up, the little tree clung to the rocky cliff. The wind never stopped blowing, and many times the tree shivered in the cold ocean spray. One day, a new group of birds stopped to rest on the little tree. These birds sang of a wondrous place where the mountains stretched towards the sky and everywhere you looked there were beautiful trees with fat, thick needles. They sighed with pleasure as they remembered the sweet smell of pine that filled the air. "Now those are real trees!" exclaimed the birds. "Why aren't you more like them?" the birds taunted.

"I can't," sobbed the little tree, "I just can't!"

The years came and went. The little tree bent his head to the wind, and bent still further when the gales stormed hard around him. His heart was very sad, because he could not be with the majestic trees that sank their roots into the rich, black earth of the far away forests. All he could do was cling to the cliff and endure the wind.

One day, after many, many years had come and gone, a very strange thing happened. It was a sunny day, and for once, the wind from the ocean was gentle and soft. The little tree was breathing peacefully beneath the clear blue sky. Suddenly, the quiet of the drowsy afternoon was broken. "Mommy! Daddy! Look at this tree. Isn't it the wonderfulest tree you've ever seen?"

"Yes, darling. Yes, it is. Just look at those beautiful curves in its trunk."

"Take my picture! Take my picture with this tree!"

The little tree couldn't believe his ears. But there, right against his gnarled trunk, snuggled a beaming little boy waiting proudly for his picture to be taken.

"How did the tree get to be like this, Daddy?" the little boy asked.

"Well, son, this is a very strong tree. It hasn't had an easy life perched way up here on the cliff. When this tree was just a baby, the wind kept blowing against it, until its trunk twisted round and round. You can tell it is a very brave tree. Look up and down this coast. You don't see many trees, do you? Most of them couldn't survive. But this one did. And it's just magnificent, isn't it."

"It is. And do you know what? When I get home, I'm going to tell all my friends about this wonderful tree. I'm going to tell them to visit it."

The boy's father and mother just smiled. But the boy kept his promise. Much to the little tree's amazement, other families came to visit; more and more of them every week. And everyone who came, admired the little tree and took many, many pictures.

Now, even though the wind still blows and the ocean spray drenches the little tree, he doesn't mind. He is filled with joy and filled with pride that so many people come to visit. He isn't lonely any more. Now, when the birds come to rest on his twisted back, they sing—not of the far away forests—but of the strength, the courage and the beauty of the little tree.

# TAKING A CHANCE

We made a decision—my son, my husband and I. Against the best and well-intentioned advice of experts, we decided to try the new, more academically-oriented school. The transition from the cocoon of special education to the new high school was not easy or problem free. But Rob did what he had done so many times before—risen to the challenge, struggled, endured—and grown and blossomed and matured.

I made another decision as well. As a moral principle, I would not subject Rob to any more standardized tests. For, whatever the tests measure, it is not the courage and faith and hope that allow an 11-year-old boy to leave everything and everyone he has ever known to live with strangers in an unknown city in a distant state.

# LOVE IS NOT ENOUGH

When Earl and I had started seriously pursuing the idea of adoption, we were quite lucky to get connected with an Adoptive Parent Support Group. We were like sponges, soaking up the stories and experiences of the families who had already been through the process of adoption and were now "old hands" at the parenting business. Early on, one message came through loud and clear, "Love is not enough!" It seems that in the olden days of adoption, parents and professionals often believed that love would be enough to "fix" the problems that children, battered by life's misfortunes, bring into their new families. "This," these adoption pros declared in no uncertain terms, "is not so!" Being a quick and skillful learner, I got the message. Love is not enough and so, as conscientious and enlightened parents, Earl and I should draw upon all available resources to help our child overcome the adversity of his past and prepare himself for a healthier, happier future.

From the moment I met the directors of the alternative high school that Robby ultimately attended, I knew that we had finally found the educational resource that had been eluding us. These people seemed to work magic with teenagers who, for a variety of reasons, had come to hate school. They did more than teach math, English, science and history. By ignoring the arbitrary trappings of SCHOOL (dress codes, gum chewing, swearing, busy-work) and focusing on each student's unique talents and needs, they ameliorated the effects of mis-educative experiences and rekindled in their students a love of learning. This is what I desperately wanted for Rob, to cherish learning as I do. My faith and hope were rekindled.

※

The report card periods at Rob's high school were eight weeks long. At the four week mark, mid-term grade reports were issued. So every four weeks I "got a reading" on Rob's progress; not just his grades in any particular course, but progress on the more fundamental and important issue of his coming to value learning. My new found hope dwindled each time I saw the "incomplete" grades and read the notes. "Rob needs to pay attention in class. Rob is capable of doing the work, but he hasn't turned in any of his assignments."

Now others might say, "What kind of parent are you? Didn't you make Rob sit down and do his homework? Didn't you keep in touch with the school to make sure he was doing his work? Didn't you give him rewards for work accomplished, for good grades? Didn't you set up logical consequences when he goofed off? Didn't you offer to help him when he got stuck? Didn't you make him set aside a specific time and place to study? Didn't you explain to him how he needs to study so he can get ahead in life?"

Yes! **Yes! Yes!** Over the years, Earl and I had tried all of that and more. We set up system upon system upon system. And each time, Rob found the cracks in the system faster than we could fill them. It came down to a simple reality. The more we tried to make him perform in school, the more we reinforced the lessons of his mis-educative experience, learning is painful and hateful. The more we focused on the importance of education, the more Rob focused on his goal of avoiding anything and everything that had to do with school.

At last, we set forth a simple plan. "Rob," we said, "if you get C's and better, you get to keep television and VCR privileges. If you get anything lower, the TV's disconnected until you bring your grades up. It's up to you, and we are not going to nag you about your school work. We'll find out how you're doing at mid- and end-term. Let us know if you want our help with anything."

Having lived with Rob for five years, it came as no surprise that he continued to watch television and ignore school work. So, when his midterm grades came, I was prepared for the incompletes, Ds and Fs. I tried to find something positive to say and then mentioned as neutrally as possible that Earl would disconnect the television when he got home from work.

Rob protested. I took a breath, tried to remain calm, and reminded him of the conditions we had set.

"Well, that's a stupid rule!" he grumbled, contempt tinging his voice.

"Maybe so, but it's the one you agreed to."

"No I didn't. It's what you and Dad set up." The disparagement dripped from his mouth.

"Ok, Dad and I set the conditions. We happen to think it's important for you to get an education."

"Why?" he challenged with all of the disdain only a self-righteous teenager can muster. "So, I can end up like you and Dad? Working all the time like idiots!" He stomped away, dismissing me with his words and his footsteps.

I lost it. Then and there, all of the rage that had been simmering beneath the despair, disappointment and desperation erupted. For an eternity, I screamed at Rob and catalogued in minute detail each and every flaw in his character. If he hadn't towered over me by several inches, I would have picked him up and smashed him through the nearest wall. (I think that Dewey would have labeled this a mis-educative interaction, but quite frankly, I didn't give a damn!)

It was when I noticed the spit flying from my lips that I finally backed off. "I'm so enraged, I'm frothing at the mouth," I thought. Shaking and sobbing, I locked myself in my bedroom. "This is crazy, absolutely crazy. I want so much for him, but I end up hurting him." Never had I felt so hopeless or helpless.

I called a friend of mine who specializes in counseling abusive men and arranged a time to meet with him. As soon as I entered his office, I resumed my rantings and ravings. He waited patiently until I finally wound down, and he then asked, "What are you afraid of?"

That gave me pause. "That he'll never make anything of himself," I said at last. "That he'll expect the world to give to him, or worse yet, that he's entitled to take whatever he wants without working for it."

"Why does that frighten you so much?" my friend probed further.

"From as early as I can remember," I sobbed, the tears welling up again, "I have been programmed to believe that you work for what you want. You study hard; you work hard, and you make something of yourself. I'm giving Rob a chance for that, and he keeps throwing it away. I can't stand it anymore!"

"Maybe what you're afraid of is wanting for yourself what Rob seems to have. The freedom to play, the freedom to be irresponsible."

"But life isn't like that. I mean you just can't go through life like Conan the Barbarian, pillaging and plundering!"

"Is Rob like that?"

"No," I grudgingly admitted. "But that's my catastrophic fantasy."

I left my friend's office a little while later, having calmed down enough to take a stab at rational thought. Driving home, I continued to think about Conan the Barbarian. Suddenly, a new image emerged, The Incredible Hulk, complete with voice over, ". . .unleashed the raging beast within. . ."

"Was this how I seem to Rob?" I wondered. One minute a seemingly calm and reasonable person, the next a raving lunatic. The image expanded and I saw the marquis, our names in lights:

## CONAN THE BARBARIAN VS. THE INCREDIBLE HULK

A day or so later, I suggested that Rob use his considerable artistic talent to create two customized T-shirts. One would have a picture of The Incredible Hulk; the other Conan The Barbarian.

"From now on," I explained, "whenever we're on the verge of a fight, which ever one of us has more presence of mind will shout out "T-shirts." We'll both take a time out to don our shirts and then if we can still keep a straight face, we'll continue with the argument."

"Right, Mom," Rob agreed with a look and tone that clearly said I'd lost my mind.

Rob did, however, humor me, halfway. Several days later, he presented me with a green T-shirt emblazoned with the scowling visage of The Incredible Hulk. After a year had gone by, he had yet to do Conan The Barbarian.

In the aftermath of my vicious tantrum, I did a lot of soul searching. With Earl's help and the help of some very good friends, I came at last to three realizations. First, the one value I had never even thought to examine during those home study exercises was my family's legacy about education and learning.

Second, there was literally nothing in heaven and earth that I could do to make Rob accept this legacy as his. Whatever learning means to me, it does not mean the same thing to Rob, and I am powerless to change that.

Third, knowing this, knowing that our family legacies clash at the most fundamental level, I had a choice. I could reject him for what he is not, or accept and love him for what he is.

The words of the Adoptive Parent Support Group came back to me. Love is not enough. Maybe so. But, maybe, just maybe, in the final analysis, love is all that really matters.

# EPILOGUE

A few years after Rob left home (or was thrown out of the house as he prefers to put it), I was sitting with several close friends at a Panera Restaurant. Between bites of Fuji apple salad, I looked up and said, "I've come to the realization that I'm a complete failure as a mother."

"Oh no!" they were quick to reply and rushed in with a number of well-meant reassurances that I had been a more than adequate parent. While I appreciated their kind comments, they missed the point. Far from being devastated by this self-assessment, I felt liberated. I was free from the ambition to be a better mother than mine had been. I was free from the need to prove that my approach to parenting was right and my husband's was wrong. I was free of the fear that Rob might say someday, "You really screwed up. You were an awful mother." I was free to say, "You're right. I didn't mean to be and I tried hard to be a good mom. But I know I failed you and I'm sorry." My acceptance of failure was, as the Twelve-Step folks say, "hitting bottom." The crash-landing swept away false pride, smugness, self-righteous anger, and the illusion of control. I became a grateful recovering know-it-all. Of course, recovery is never a fully realized state of grace. It is an on-going process of vigilance against the temptation to impose my reality on others. It is a constant reminder that I can walk with someone on his or her life journey, but I cannot dictate what that journey must be.

The line between "walking with" versus dictating the course of a child's life-journey is a tricky one. As a parent, I want what is best for my son. I want to keep him safe from danger; protect him from heartache; provide opportunities for a successful and meaningful life. Given my age, life-experience, and education, I thought Rob should defer (acquiesce) to my views on the path to successful adulthood. When neither incentives nor punishments resulted in compliance, I labeled him as defiant and came to a moment when I said (to myself, if not aloud), "Okay. You think you know so much go live your own way. See how that turns out." At the time, I was angry and spiteful. Later, in accepting failure, in hitting bottom, in becoming a grateful recovering know-it-all, I acknowledged a fundamental, existential reality—no one (not even the most loving parent) can dictate the terms of another's life. That is the reason I try to curb my impulse for advice-giving. I have, nevertheless, pondered several issues that might also confound other parents. I share these here, not as absolute truths, but as points for consideration.

In my early days as an adoptive parent, I joined with several other adoptive moms, an expert in special-needs adoption, and a nationally recognized expert in child development to study the issue of attachment. At that time, most of the literature focused on attachment between birth mothers and their babies. We wanted to explore what attachment might look like between adopted children and their adoptive parents—especially in cases of older child adoptions where children had spent several years with birth parents before being removed by departments of child welfare. Research had suggested that even very young infants exhibit one of three patterns of attachment: secure attachment, insecure attachment, and avoidant attachment. Secure attachment is grounded in trust between a helpless infant and its caregiver (typically the mother). When the baby's needs are met, trust develops along with a sense that the world is a safe and nurturing place. This lays a healthy foundation for subsequent stages of development.

As a study group, we speculated that attachment would be complicated for older children who, because of birth parent neglect or abuse, had come into the foster system and were subsequently adopted. In all likelihood, they would not have a sense of trust and security; they would probably see the world as a dangerous place. Yet, even in cases where attachment is insecure or avoidant, the emotional bonds between children and their birth parents are not easily severed. Children can enter adoptive families with mixed feelings of love, loyalty, and anger toward birth parents; mistrust of adults; fear of the world. Having been victimized by birth parents, they may feel victimized again by a bureaucracy that has taken them away from everything they knew and placed them with strangers in unfamiliar surroundings. Given such circumstances, what does it mean to parent lovingly and responsibly?

While I might not have had an answer to that question, I did believe that I could take classes and read books that would provide an answer. One recurring theme was the importance of natural consequences versus punishment. The parenting principle was to give children choices and let them learn from the consequences of their choice. Wise choices resulted in positive consequences; "bad" choices resulted in unpleasant outcomes. Through experience, children would learn to make wise choices. The logic of this approach seemed unassailable. The first hint of trouble came when I gave Rob a choice and he responded, "I don't want either of those choices. I want a third one." The trouble escalated when Rob's choice was not to study, failed most of his courses, and launched a verbal assault when I tried to impose the consequence of "no television until grades improved."

Here's the crack in the foundation of the natural-consequences principle of parenting. The <u>natural</u> consequence of not studying is ignorance. Failing grades are an artificial consequence. Revocation of television privileges is not only artificial, it is also arbitrary. Of course, as a loving, responsible parent, I saw the downside of letting Rob experience the natural consequence of his aversion to school and studying. I wanted to create a less onerous, shorter-term consequence that would nudge him in the "right" direction. This is what parents do to keep children from harm and nurture them toward competent adulthood. When, as infants, children become securely attached and trust that their parents have their best interests at heart, the imposition of artificial and even arbitrary consequences may be accepted without question. In such cases, artificial choices and consequences may serve their educative purpose.

But what happens when an infant has never experienced secure attachment? How are artificial choices and arbitrary consequences perceived by a child steeped in mistrust of parents and, in turn, other adult authority figures like teachers? Do they experience the "natural consequences" has thinly veiled punishments? Is "defiance" actually resistance to perceived manipulation? If so, toward whom is the resistance directed—birth parents who proved themselves unworthy of trust or adoptive parents whose trustworthiness is yet to be proven? These questions prompt me to ponder the related issue of punishment and rewards.

If insecurely or avoidantly attached children interpret artificial choices and arbitrary consequences as punishments, can rewards be an incentive to induce compliance with parental expectations? In essence, a promised reward entails a *quid pro quo* bargain. When the child does behavior "x," reward "y" will follow, thereby engendering motivation to engage in the rewarded behavior. Such behavioral conditioning works quite well and predictably with pigeons and rats. It is the basis of the contracts generated in behavioral therapy programs and special education classes. It is the rationale behind the charts where stars for "good behavior" are accumulated in anticipation of an eventual reward. Like the idea of natural consequences, "behavior management" sounds logical. Through a system of rewards, a child gradually learns to manage his own behavior. Unless the rewards hold no meaning for him. Unless the payoff for good behavior is too remote to counteract the need for immediate gratification—regardless of the price that will be paid for impulsivity. Unless mistrust undermines faith that the reward will ever be given. Unless the *quid pro quo* bargain was coerced by authority figures with all the power.

On a family vacation to San Francisco, we toured Alcatraz Prison. When we came to the cells that had been used for solitary confinement, the guide said, "There was no light in these cells. The only human contact came when food was slid through a slot in the door. Some prisoners would tear a button off their shirt, toss it into the air, and then grope around until they found it and then do it all over again. That was their way of staying sane." This is a stunning case study in the futility of punishments and rewards taken to an extreme most of us can hardly imagine. Compliance with prison rules would result in the "reward" of escaping a pitch-black cell with nothing to do but search the floor for a button. Defiance resulted in solitary, inhumane punishment. What would cause a man to remain defiant? Did mental illness make him incapable of acting in his own best interest? Did surrendering control to external authority represent a fundamental and unacceptable loss of self? Do well-intentioned reward systems represent a micro-version of this battle for control over one's life?

The analogy, some might say, is ridiculous. Loving parents, committed therapists, caring teachers are hardly the same as prison guards. Behavioral management systems will help children develop skills that are necessary for a happy, productive life. I forget whether Rob was in his late 20s or early 30s when he told me that all of the special education classes, all of the therapy sessions made him feel that he wasn't good enough for us. I thought we were sending the message, "You were cheated out of a childhood that would have allowed you to flourish. You are bright and talented. We are giving you the opportunity to 'catch up,' to regain what should have been your natural birthright." The message he heard was, "You are a flawed, imperfect human being who isn't good enough for us. We are going to fix you until you are acceptable in our eyes." Within this frame is it fair to think of his resistance to rewards and consequences (punishments) as defiance? Might his resistance be interpreted more fairly as a valiant battle to hold true to his sense of self?

In concert with the whole reward/consequences system of parenting comes another principle, namely the importance of consistency. Consistency provides structure that children need to feel safe and secure. Consistency allows children to know what is expected and to feel successful when their behavior brings about the expected outcome. Consistency requires tough love. For some time, I thought tough love meant upping the stakes: imposing more severe consequences to force the "right choice." Then at a parent support meeting, a mother described the night she came home and found her alcoholic son curled up on her back porch. This was after years of failed rehabilitation attempts, repeated lapses in recovery, innumerable false promises made and broken. She realized that she could not save him from his addiction. He would have to do that for himself; if he wanted to. So that night she did the hardest thing she had ever done. She stepped over her son, went into the house, and locked the door. That's when I finally understood. Tough love wasn't a manipulative parenting technique. I was wrong to think about being tough on Rob. It was I who wasn't tough enough to accept Rob's right to live life on his own terms, even if those terms seemed self-defeating from my point of view.

Years after Rob and I had arrived at a state of détente, I read *Far from the Tree: Parents, Children, and the Search for Identity* by Andrew Solomon. In the introduction to the book, Solomon states:

> Because of the transmission of identity from one generation to the next, most children share at least some traits with their parents. These are *vertical* identities. Attributes and values are passed down from parent to child across the generations not only through strands of DNA, but also through shared cultural norms.[1]

When we had initially read Rob's psycho-social history, we were cautious about our ability to be the kind of parents he needed. But one line caught my attention and won me over, "Rob probably has the ability to go to college." This line contributed to the idea that

---

[1] Solomon, Andrew. *Far from the Tree: Parents, Children, and the Search for Identity*. New York: Scribner, 2012, p. 2.

we could restore to Rob what he had been cheated out of in his birth family. College-educated was in the cultural DNA of both my husband's family and mine; it was an identity we wanted to transmit to the next generation. However, as I wrote in the story, "Love is not Enough":

> ...the one value I had never even thought to examine during those home study exercises was my family's legacy about education and learning. . . [and] there was literally nothing in heaven and earth that I could do to make Rob accept this legacy as his. Whatever learning means to me, it does not mean the same thing to Rob, and I am powerless to change that.

I learned from reading *Far from the Tree* that when Rob's life intersected with mine, we brought into proximity two different vertical identities. This set the stage for a struggle for identity that I was inadequately prepared to help Rob navigate. In hindsight, I doubt that any of the special education teachers or our family therapist was adequately prepared. Just how unprepared we were came home to me when I read *Hillbilly Elegy* by J.D. Vance.[2] As Vance talked about his roots in the Appalachian Mountain culture of the South and the dynamics in his family, he could have been talking about Rob's. Vance wrote quite poignantly about the circumstances that led to his attending Yale University Law School and how he still feels caught between the culture he was born to and the culture he joined. In spite of all he has accomplished, he still struggles with questions: Who am I, really? Where do my loyalties lie? Have I betrayed my past?

Reading Vance's memoir against the backdrop of *Far from the Tree* underscored the profoundly painful and complicated identity struggle that Rob faced. Through no fault of his own and without

---

2  Vance, J.D. *Hillbilly Elegy: A Memoir of a Family and Culture in Crisis.* New York: HarperCollins, 2016.

his consent, Child Welfare Services cut Rob off from the vertical lines of his identity. Well-meaning case workers and we, as well-meaning adoptive parents, naively believed that we could graft into him new vertical lines of cultural DNA. Prevailing adoption wisdom at the time espoused the notion that appropriate educational and therapeutic services would help the graft to take. We were wrong. The termination of his birth parents' rights was undoubtedly justified, but that action set in motion a cascade of events that ultimately Rob, and only Rob, could make sense of. His vertical identity was no longer firmly rooted in the Appalachian soil of his birth. Nor did it re-root in the soil of his adoptive family. Growing into adulthood meant coming to terms with competing lines of vertical identity. What did he want to accept? What did he want to reject? Who did he want to be? What did he want to become?

I don't know if I could have walked with Rob on his journey to sort through those questions. Perhaps if I had been wiser, I might have. It is just as likely that I would have continued in my know-it-all fashion to try to control or manipulate the outcome. Regardless, I cannot turn back the clock and retrace the journey with deeper understanding. I can only say I am glad that Rob, like a battle-worn Ulysses, found his way back home. I hope he knows how much I respect the strength and courage it took for him to journey this far. His journey continues, and I hope he knows my love goes with him on the path ahead.

## Learning Moments Press

Learning Moments Press is an independent publishing company dedicated to sharing the wisdom that comes from thoughtful reflection on experience. The Wisdom of Life Series offers insightful reflections on significant life events that challenge the meaning of one's life, one's sense of self, and one's place in the world.

Cooligraphy artist Daniel Nie created the logo for Learning Moments Press by combining two symbol systems. Following the principles of ancient Asian symbolism, Daniel framed the logo with the initials of Learning Moments Press. Within this frame, he has replicated the Adinkra symbol for *Sankofa* as interpreted by graphic artists at the Documents and Designs Company. As explained by Wikipedia, Adinkra is a writing system of the Akan culture of west Africa. *Sankofa* symbolizes taking from the past what is good and bringing it into the present in order to make positive progress through the benevolent use of knowledge. Inherent in this philosophy is the belief that the past illuminates the present and that the search for knowledge is a life-long process.

www.ingramcontent.com/pod-product-compliance
Lightning Source LLC
Chambersburg PA
CBHW052134010526
44113CB00036B/2258